Words
from the
heart

Joe Al Green

PAGE PUBLISHING, INC.
New York, NY

First originally published by Page Publishing, Inc. 2018

ISBN 978-1-64350-864-1 (Paperback)
ISBN 978-1-64350-866-5 (Hardcover)
ISBN 978-1-64350-865-8 (Digital)

Printed in the United States of America

It Happens in Life

It seems funny, it would appear
That I started my life late last year.
You see, the doctor told me I had the big C,
And I hope the Lord will have mercy on me.

I wasted my time all through my life
And have nothing to show
for it, not even a wife.
I've worked hard; I've done it on my own
Just to realize, now I'm all alone.

I looked in the mirror, and what did I see?
Just an old gray-haired man
looking back at me.

As I walk through the valley
with despair, I do descend.
I ask myself, have I been a good
person or bad person?
I cannot comprehend.
Do you think of me? Do you see me?

Do you hear me when I speak?
O Lord, I pray to you.
It's your blessing that I seek.

And if I see you with your thorny crown
Who walks upon your hallowed ground,
I shall ask you to guide me to the light.
I shall gladly die with delight.

Photo Album

We lost a loved one the other day,
So everyone bent their head to pray.
There are days when you feel
blue, when the sky is gray,
Then you look in an album and
see pictures of kids at play.
There are pictures of days gone by;
I wish I could relive them, I cannot lie.
A person would have to be totally blind
If you could not see memories frozen in time.
There are pictures of Grandma,
Grandpa, or Mom and Dad,
Or your favorite uncle that
makes you feel sad.
You see pictures of people that
are tattered and old,
Of family and friends that
you don't even know.
You hang on to pictures that
are dear to your heart,

And if you could bring one person
back, where would you start?
So please, take a picture of me frozen in time,
So I can be remembered, if
you would be so kind.

Dorothy Jean Green

There were times she looked so frail
But everyone knew she was tough as nails
In her house, there was always
an extra place at the table
And she would find you a place
to sleep if you weren't able

But the one thing I admired the most
That she held her family so close
Her heart was so big and full of love
So when she showed her humanity,
it fit her like a glove

But she was raised that way, don't you see
She was taught to care for
everyone, even you and me
When her family was around, this
would put a smile upon her face
And if her grandkids were there,
the smile would stay in place

She made her peace with God so long ago
And she was ready to go, or
at least she hoped so
Despair, discomfort, and pain
Have poured down on her like a falling rain

For weeks now she has been
saying her goodbyes
She knew when her time comes, she
would have to sever her human ties
She has been a sister, an aunt,
a mother, and a wife
She has been these things most of her life

She is not with us on this day
But I can almost hear her say
For all those whom I love
I will watch over you from above

Oscar's Poem

I was born into the Green clan,
To a simple woman and a simple man.
They taught me how to work hard
And do the best you can.
So I lived a simple life
With three kids and a beautiful wife.
My mom taught me how to love
life and everything in it.
My dad taught me how to live life for, at
times, it may seem to last only a minute.
I have a regret, it's that I didn't
get to say goodbye.
This saddens my heart, I cannot lie.
But I do want to see something
that I will adore;
That is the gate to the kingdom of the Lord.
It is the Lord and family that
has passed before me,
This is whom I want to see.
I can almost hear them say, "For
you, we saved a place in line."

I will say, "As long as I'm with
you, any place is fine."
People are afraid of things they
cannot see; they fear it.
But now I am only here in spirit.
I am here but cannot be seen.
My name is Oscar Lee Green.

Debbie's Wings

When she was brought into this world,
LeMasters were told they had
a beautiful baby girl.
She was loved by all; that's what they say.
Things were fine until one sad day.
She was caught in a fire. She was set ablaze.
She endured the pain, and
everyone was amazed.
She held her head high, and
she had her spirit.
She embraced the will for life
when others would fear it.
She did not know what life would bring,
But she wanted to experience it just the same.
There were ups and downs in
life she had to endure;
She knew she could make it through
because her spirit was pure.
She was born Debra Kay LeMaster,
and she was blessed.
She endured life. You see, that was her test.

She has earned her angel's
wings; she is in flight.
She has left us now, and we
think of her every night.

Memories

When my time comes, will
there be any regrets
Of things I have done that I didn't forget?
Or are singing angels what I will hear?
Or nothing, just darkness, that's what I fear.
Will I take my memories that are so strong,
Or will my mind be wiped
clean, and all will be gone?
I hope that this is not the case.
Why, because I have so many
memories; let me give you a taste.
Like fishing at the lake with my dad;
Man, that made me so glad.
Or when my mom said just
wait till you have kids;
That's funny because that's just what I did.
Or is it the simple things I
will miss the most,
Like sitting in the kitchen with my
wife having coffee and toast?

Or just seeing my grandkids, these are
the things I shall miss the most.
Are there bad memories? Oh
yes, there are some.
So live to the fullest, for
tomorrow may never come.

The Last Day

I look into the misty morning haze,
Thinking of the past; those were the days.
As kids, we were told to go out and play.
We would do just that all through the day.
As we grow older, we lose loved
ones along the way.
We feel the pain and the
sorrow, what can I say?
We learn life is filled with good and bad.
That's the way it is; please don't feel sad.
My heart is burdened by the pain for the loss.
We learn life goes on; that is the cost.
I know my day will come
when I leave this earth,
Flying so fast and high into the universe.
Now I sit here old and gray,
Awaiting my last breath up on my last day.
Will I remember the time I
cherish the most of that day?
They told me to go out and play,
And we did just that all the day!

Daddy

I was on my way to the school bus
When I got the news you had left us.
I can still hear your voice in
the back of my mind,
Telling me everything is going to be just fine.
But I didn't get to tell you goodbye;
Now all I can do is sit here and cry.
There were times you'd step in
To make my life all right again.
I remember things you'd do and say,
Like "At bedtime, you kids better pray."
Sky-blue eyes, smile so bright,
I love you, Daddy, hugs, good night.
Playing your guitar for family and friends,
And cooking barbecue on the weekends;
Campfires on the riverbanks;
So many wonderful memories, I say thanks.
Sky-blue eyes, smile so bright,
I love you, Daddy, hugs, good night.
I wish you could have watched my kids grow.
I know you would be proud, don't you know.

Well, I am done with my prayers for tonight.
Time to close my eyes, hope
you come into sight.
One last thing before I go;
It's something you already know.
Sky-blue eyes, smile so bright,
I love you, Daddy, hugs, good night.

Why

John's phone was ringing. He opened his eyes and wondered who would dare call him this early in the morning, when he planned to sleep late—his first weekend off in six months.

He picked up the phone and said, "This better be good!"

His friend Mark said, "Man, we have not seen you in months. We're all going to the beach today. Why don't you come along?"

John thought for a moment, *Yeah, that's what I need to do, go to the beach and have all the good-looking girls look at my white, pasty, bony legs, and I will probably get sunburned.*

Mark said, "Dude, you need to come. We are talking about taking a road trip. You'll have a great time."

Now there's an idea. *A vacation, now that's what I need.*

"Sounds good," John said, "I'll jump in the shower then head that way."

Mary was looking for flip-flops to wear to the beach. She went to her catch all rooms, looked in the corner, and there they were, not her flip-flops, but Brad's boots. She thought for a moment. Well, that's the only thing he forgot, and he will miss them. You see, two months ago, Brad came home and gathered all his things and was loading them in the car when Mary pulled in the driveway.

She got out of her car and said, "What's up?"

He just kept loading his car, and over his shoulder, he said, "Got to be in Ohio Monday. I have a new job," then just got in his car and drove away.

Just like that. Why? She wanted an explanation. You would think after a couple of years together, he would explain why. But when she tried to call him, the recording said it was no longer in service. But after thinking about it for a while, she thought, *Hell, he wasn't in service when he was here anyway.*

Mary was slim and trim, and she needed a tan. So when her friends invited her to the beach, she said yes.

John and Mary's friends all knew each other, so no introductions were made; but John didn't know Mary, and he was sure he wanted to know her or at least talk to her. But every time he got near her, he couldn't speak. He felt like a schoolboy. He would look at her blond hair and blue eyes, and it would take his breath away. He couldn't think. He wanted to break the ice with her, say something, hell, anything. He didn't know Mary was having the same problem.

When she saw John at the ice chest, she saw her opening. She ran up to the ice chest and said, "Hi, I'm thirsty."

John looked at her and replied, "Hi, thirsty, my name is John." They both laughed.

Mary looked into his eyes, and when he looked back into her blue eyes, he noticed a tear roll down her cheek. It took a long moment before he started to panic. *Why did I say something so stupid?* he thought. "If I said something or did something wrong, I am truly sorry."

She saw the concern on his face and said, "You didn't say or do anything wrong."

A little puzzled, John said then, "Why? Why do you cry?"

She thought to herself, she had been waiting for this moment all her life, but she didn't say that to

John. What she did say was, "It would take all day to explain, and I don't think you would understand."

John just blinked and said, "Okay."

They were together every day after that. After several months, while taking a walk, John was amazed how easy it was to talk to her, and she was thinking how safe and comfortable she was with him.

John said, "When I met you, I had a hole in my chest where my heart should be. Since then, you have filled it. I love you."

She looked at him with tears in her eyes, and he said, "Why are you crying?"

She wiped the tears away and said, "You wouldn't understand."

Then she said, "This may sound funny, but I have been waiting for you all my life. I love you too."

He reached a hand out to her. She went to take it. When she looked into the palm of his hand, there was a ring. She jumped up and down and said, "Yes, yes, yes."

He said, "I need to ask first."

She said, "No, you don't," and kissed him.

A year or so after the wedding, she wanted to have a picnic in the park. John was sitting on a blanket, telling her one of his jokes about two blondes driving around the lake with their top down, when they drove into the lake and drowned because they couldn't get the door unlocked. That is one reason she loved him so much, because he made her laugh.

He was looking at the tears on her face and asked, "Why do you cry?"

She just smiled and said, "You wouldn't understand."

Out of nowhere a puppy ran up and jumped in her lap. She said, "How cute," and hugged the pup.

John said, "No, no, no way. We don't need a dog."

She said, "Okay. We need to find its owner then."

They walked around and asked everyone they saw if the pup was theirs. Their replies were "No," "No way," or "Not my dog."

John looked at Mary. She had tears rolling down her cheeks and said, "No way. We don't need a dog."

He looked at her once more then said, "Okay, might as well take him home. After all, we already have a name for him." She looked puzzled. John said, "No way. We will name him No Way."

He watched her wipe the tears from her cheeks; it melted his heart. If he could live a thousand lives and was given a choice to live only one life, he would pick this life with her. He loved her so much.

Every day after work, he would take No Way for a walk then play with him in the front yard. Mary would sit on the top step on the porch with tears in her eyes, and he would ask why she was crying. Same answer every time: "You wouldn't understand."

One night at dinner, she asked, "Would you like to have children?"

He said, "Yes."

Then she said, "I will go see a doctor and find out why we don't have one yet."

The next night, he came home to find her crying. He walked up and put his arms around her and said, "What did the doctor say?"

She said, "Kids were the least of her problems. The doctor said he would run the tests but was sure I would not be on this earth much longer. He said around six months."

Well, the months turned into weeks, the weeks turned into days, and the days turned into hours. In her hospital room, sharing their last moments together, she said, "You have to promise me something."

John said, "Whatever you want."

She said, "Promise me after I go, you go find No Way a girlfriend."

John looked at her face for a moment and said, "Okay. Is there a hidden message there?"

She just smiled and said, "Maybe," with a smile on her face, then she squeezed his hand. He looked down at her hand and squeezed back. But when he looked up at her face, she was gone.

Eight or nine months later, John woke to the ringing of the phone. He answered it. It was Mark.

"Hey, dude. Let's go to the beach."

John said, "No, don't feel like it."

Mark said, "Dude, you need to get on with the rest of your life. I mean, I'm sorry for your loss, but, dude."

John smiled to himself. "No, dude. You are right. Talk to you later."

John got up, took himself a shower, dressed, went to the pound with No Way, and let No Way pick himself a girlfriend.

He put his house up for sale and started looking for a new place. When he found what he was looking for, he went home to pack. As he was sorting through their things, he found a notebook. Taped to the front of it was a note. It said, "John, for you. It will explain everything. Love, Mary."

He held his breath for a moment and thought, *Do I want to know what's in it? Sure I do, but what if she cheated on me or found out she was on the run? Maybe she did something wrong.* But he wanted to see what was in it.

He wanted to read the last entry first, so he flipped it over and opened it. It was blank. His heart sank, then he flipped the next page forward, and it was blank. He kept flipping forward until the first page, and on it were these words that brought tears to his eyes.

"From the first day at the ice chest, I knew I loved you, and every time I think of how much I loved you, it made me cry. So now you know the reason why. Love, Mary."

Midnight Lover

She comes over late at night,
But she'll be gone by the morning light.
She likes to keep me in her world.
My midnight lover, she's my girl.
Not really sure how we came to be,
But at night she devotes her time to me.
On rainy nights, when the lightning strikes,
She'll cover her head and hold me tight.
At times she's playful like a little girl;
That's why I need this girl in my world.
Summer nights we lie in the
grass and stare at the stars.
We are happy and content, at least so far.
She likes to keep me in her world.
My midnight lover, she's my girl.
Not quite sure how this story will end,
Because I'm not really sure how it began.
The night we met, it was supposed
to be a one-night stand,
But we danced late into the night
to the music of the band.

Don't know if she's married or has another,
I'm afraid to ask. I may not
like what I discover.
I'm at a point to make her a proposition,
But I'm worried of the
outcome of her decision.
I want to keep this girl in my world.
She's my midnight lover. She's my girl.

My Dear

I remember the first day you said, "Hello."
I was not sure how things would go.
As I look back into our past,
I did not know if our love would last.
That day you walked into my life,
I knew I would ask you to be my wife.
We have worked on our love
all through the years.
We had good and bad times
and, yes, even tears.
We had two kids; it made us a family of four.
It was your love and devotion
for them that I adore.
Maybe things didn't work out
like we had planned,
But we built a family and a
house upon our own land.
Now the kids have been gone for so long.
Damn, baby, where has the time gone?
But here we are, old and gray.
Decades later, what can I say?

I do not know why I feel my end is near,
But because of you, I do not fear.
The thing I will miss most
Is lying in bed, holding you close.
So when I'm there and you are here,
I want to make one thing perfectly clear:
I will be waiting on the other side, my dear.
So once more I will be able to hold you near.

One Sunny Day

Looking out the window at the pouring rain,
Watching raindrops upon my windowpane.
Memories of you rushing through my brain.
No matter what I do, it will
never be the same.
I remember a day walking down the avenue.
The streets were full, but it
was just me and you.
I don't know what to do.
I have only myself to blame.
You said I hurt you, and it made you blue
By the little things that I would say and do.
Was it really you
When you said that we're through?
Well, I remember a sunny
day when you said,
With me, you wanted to grow old and gray.
You left me speechless with nothing to say,
And I will never forget that sunny day.
It's a relationship that didn't last.

Now you're a shadow that
you can no longer cast.
I know I can't live in the past,
So it looks like rain in my forecast.
You're now a shadow in the
doorway of my mind;
A love so sweet that I can no longer find.
I wish for a button that I
could push and play
So I won't lose that memory
of that one sunny day.

Why

You ask me why I cry.
Well, let me tell you why.
I think you need to know
Where our love could go.
There are times you treat me so bad;
That makes me feel so sad.
My love for you is so strong,
But you've known that all along.
I do know that you care.
I see it in the time we share.
I am not ready to throw our love away,
But at times, you leave me
speechless with nothing to say.
There are times you make me so crazy
I don't know what to do,
But then your love is like the morning sun;
It comes shining through.
There's a thin line between love and hate.
At times, I wonder what will be our fate.

I love you so much; this is why I cry,
But if I leave now, will you
know the reason why?

New Fallen Snow

As we watch the sunset
On new fallen snow,
Our newfound love
Will just grow and grow.
We were friends then
Lovers then husband and wife,
But I vow to stick by your side
For the rest of your life.
We said our vows
In front of family and friends.
We will be husband and wife till the end.
We shall start a family
Where once there was none.
A family we shall have
When we are done.
While we are young, we will have
children—one, two, maybe three.
As we grow old,
We watch them grow,
Then we will set them free.
We have come full circle. How do I know?

Because we sit on our porch and
watch our grandkids play
On the new fallen snow.

The Letter

As I sit here watching the
day turn into night,
I think of all the times that I held you tight.
You said you loved me; it broke my heart.
So many things to tell you. Where do I start?
You see, baby, I am always
scheming and up to no good.
I'm not like everyone else and do
the right things I should.
I am the hard and ugly guy with no feelings,
Don't know why you found me so appealing.
You are a prim and proper young
woman; that's a fact.
I am a bad man from the
wrong side of the tracks.
I was going to use you then push you away,
Don't know why I didn't even to this day.
You deserve loving and caring
and all that it brings.
I'm a man on the run; I can't
give you these things.

Listen close at the words I have to say.
This will hurt, but you'll forgive me one day.
This is something you don't know,
I love you so much I'm letting you go.
I want you to know you will
always be in my head.
I wrote this in a letter that I left by your bed.

Party Girl

They say she's not the girl for me.
She's been around the world, don't you see?
I don't care if she's a party girl;
I just want her in my world.
I dream of her almost every night.
My dreams of her bring much delight.
See, people don't see what I see,
But this girl wants to share
her world with me.
They say her world, I wouldn't understand.
All I see are adventures that are not planned.
Her world is filled with ups and downs,
Sometimes smiles and sometimes frowns.
Besides, it's not for you to judge,
So don't feel bad or hold a grudge.
She wants to open her world to me.
Right now, that's all I can see.
She said, "Don't you see what
you're doing to me?"
"Baby, it's the same for me, can't you see?"
She says her love, she has to defend,

But she will open her heart and let me in.
Now we share a world for both of us.
So now there is nothing left to discuss.

You and Me

Did you ever wonder where you would be
If there was no you and me?
Your life would be different in so many ways.
- Would it be like vacation
with fun-filled days?
Some people go through life like
they're playing a game.
It's funny, they're all different,
but they're all just the same.
I think it would be unjust and truly unfair
If we were to have a life that
we could not share.
It seems like our life is like
an old country song
Because my love for you has
been there all along.
Your love and your spirit is
rooted deep within my soul;
That's the way it should be, or at
least that's what I've been told.

Roberta's Rose

Jason was a small-town boy, fresh out of high school. He wanted to have fun for the summer before going to college. He had a job, well, a part-time job, for now. You see, they cut back his hours at the feedstore, but it was better than getting laid off. He is eighteen years old, has his own car, and his schooling is paid for, thanks to Dad's insurance money. He misses him so much.

You see, his dad had a heart attack and didn't make it. His mom and dad were fighting one night. It was about his mom cheating. She was yelling at his dad when his face turned red. Then that was it. Gone.

Later we found out it was from drinking and pills. Then I found out Mom's been running around for many years. You think you know a person all your life, but do you really know them? Now she's drinking and has one of her boyfriends living with us.

She didn't even take the time to ask me how I felt or if I cared. I really don't understand. Dad's only been gone six months. All this was running through his mind as he was jogging through the park.

All of a sudden, he found himself jogging out of the park heading toward Danny's soda shop. He was thinking he would get a soda to go and head for the house. As he walked in, he looked around to see the same old crowd was there. He got his soda and turned to leave when he noticed David and Belinda, with Vance and Missy behind, heading his way.

As they approached, Vance said, "You going to Cara's party tonight?"

David said, "Who you bringing?"

"No one," Jason said, "Don't want a date, just would like to spend time with my friends. That's okay with you, I hope," as he stepped aside to let the new waitress pass.

David said, "Sure it is."

Jason said, "Anyway, got to go home. So I will see you there." He turned, and out the door he went.

Jason was just a block away when a voice from behind him said, "Hey, Jason!"

He turned to see a plump girl. Wait, it was the new waitress looking at him. He was sure he had a class with her in high school but couldn't remember her name. "Yes, what can I do for you?" Jason said.

Shuffling her feet and looking a little uneasy, she said, "If you need a date, I'll go with you."

Jason said, "Well, if you heard our conversation, then why would I ask you to go?" She looked shocked. She turned and ran back toward the soda shop. He thought, *Why did I say it like that?* He said, "Wait, let me explain," but she was already going into the soda shop. He didn't want to cause a scene, so he turned and headed for home.

As he walked into the house, the first thing he saw was Ted or Todd or whatever his name was, had his mom by the hair, yelling into her face. Well, Jason lost it. He ran over, spun the guy around, and punched him in the face. It didn't even faze him. He punched Jason back and knocked him on his butt. Jason's mom jumped between them and said, "Go to your room."

Jason just looked at her and said, "But, Mom."

She said, "To your room."

He turned. She followed him. When in his room, she said, "Young man, you cool off, then go out there, and tell him you're sorry."

"What!" Jason said.

"You heard me," said his mom. He looked a little closer at her. He could tell she was drunk. She said, "You heard me. Go tell him or get out."

Jason could feel the heat of anger raise in him. He just walked over to the closet, grabbed a bag, and started packing. She turned and walked out.

When he had all he thought he needed, he walked out to his car, climbed in, looked at the house for a moment, then pulled out of the drive.

As he was passing the soda shop, he pulled over and sat there thinking, *What just happened?* In a blink of an eye, his world was upside down. He was thinking, *Forget summer.* He would go near the college he would attend, find a place to live, get a job, and get ready for school. That's when he noticed the girl sitting on the bench in front of the park just down the street. He started to turn the key to start his car when he saw he was parked in front of the florist. Flowers—that will help. He got out of his car but noticed it was closed. He saw the fake flower box filled with plastic flowers, so he grabbed one and started walking to the park.

When he reached her, he saw the hurt and the tears on her face. He said, "I am sorry," as he handed her a plastic rose. She looked at him, then at the flower, then back at him.

She said, "Is this some kind of a joke to you or what?" He wanted to explain and say he was sorry about what he said and how he said it, and about the plastic flower, but she jumped up and was gone.

He just stood there, dazed and confused, lost in the moment. He didn't understand the girl or his mom or his dad. He said to himself, "Time to go."

Now, twenty years later, here he was at the same park, parked in front of that bench. He was looking up the street. Wow, how much has changed. All the old stores were gone or boarded up, with a few new chain stores.

He had also changed. He left, a small-town boy with a few bucks in his pocket. Now at forty-four, retired with so much money, he could not spend it all in a lifetime. He was thinking he would check on his mom and maybe build a house here. It took a long time, but he did forgive her. Even though he has not seen her since he left, he's back; no fancy clothes or fancy car, just Jason.

He pulled up in front of the old hotel across Danny's, but wait, not Danny's anymore; it's Rosie's Diner. He looked at the hotel. It was a hundred years old but very nice. Still owned by the same family. He walked up to the front desk to register when the clerk said, "How long will you be staying?"

Jason said, "Let's go month by month."

The clerk said, "Okay. We have no kitchen anymore, but Rosie's is across the street, or the Supper Clubs are two blocks over."

Jason went up to his suite and unpacked. He was thinking he would go over to Rosie's, grab a bite, then go see his mom.

He walked in the door at Rosie's and was greeted by a very good-looking woman who said, "May I help you?" Jason looked around, very nice hardwood tables with high-back leather chairs. Soda shop, it was not.

"Nice place," Jason said.

She said, "Thank you. They call me Rosie. My first job was here. Later Danny sold this place to me. He turned it into a diner. I bought it, changed the sign, then remolded, but now I don't know what to call it."

Jason said, "I would leave it like it is. Makes it sound interesting."

She looked at him and said, "I know you. You're Jason, right?" They made small talk while he waited for his food. He ate then went to see his mom.

He could hardly see the house. The weeds in the front yard were so tall. He made his way to the front door and knocked, waited, then knocked again. The door opened, and an old lady said, "What do you want?"

He was about to ask to see his mom when he noticed the old drunk lady was his mom.

Jason said, "Mom, it's me, Jason."

She said, "I know who you are. I gave birth to you, stupid." He could tell she was drunk. She said, "If you need a place to stay, you know where your room is." He followed her into the living room. Newspapers and magazines were everywhere. She just looked at him for a moment then said, "They turned the electric off three months ago, and the bank is going to take the house."

Jason said, "But the house is payed for already."

She said, "Well, it was John who talked me into taking a loan out on the house. He took the money and ran. Left me holding the bag."

"Who's John?" Jason said.

His mom said, "Just a friend I partied with. He took my money, our stash, took off with some barmaid. A good thing, I don't have money for drugs now so I'm clean there. The check I get every month pays for the booze, not enough for the house payment. Are you staying? If so, you need to get a job."

"I don't need a job. I am retired now. I thought I might come back, buy some land, and build a house." He looked at her and said, "Are you going to stay drunk for the rest of your life or what?"

She snapped at him, saying, "Don't judge me." Her lower lip quivered as she looked at her son, then she said, "I am afraid to be sober. Then I would have to face what I have done in my life and yours. I'm sorry I chased you off. I said some mean things to you. No mother should ever talk to her child like that."

Jason took a deep breath, holding back tears, and said, "Mom, I love you, and if you go to rehab and sober up, I will pay the bank off and remodel the house."

They both did what they said they would do. Jason was still taking three meals a day at Rosie's and was there all the time drinking coffee. He and Rosie would have long talks. He remembered a time at one of the talks, she had made a vow to herself that she would never date a coworker or customer again. He never asked why, but he did know she was like him and had never wed.

One day they were eating lunch when she said, "How's the house coming along?"

Jason said, "Mine or Mom's?"

She said, "Yours? You mean, you are building a house? Does that mean you are going to stay?"

He said, "Yes, I'm staying. I bought the old Sutton's place, just outside of town. I am building a house on the hill next to the river. It will be a nice view."

She said, "Good for you. I'm glad."

Jason said, "May I ask you a question?"

"Sure," she said. "What is it?"

"Will you go out with me?"

She just looked at him and said, "Are you sure you want to go out with me?"

Jason smiled and said, "Yes, I would love to go out with you. Why wouldn't I?"

She said, "Do you remember this?" She reached into her pocket and pulled something out and dropped it on the table in front of him. His face went pale, and his mouth fell open. He just stared at the plastic rose in front of him.

She said, "I remember that day. It was my first day on the job here. I remember that little girl who ran up to you and asked you for a date. I have kept it all these years to remind me it's not what you say but how you say it. If someone gives you something from the heart, never refuse it. I was the little fat girl.

"So let's start over with a clean slate. Hi, my name is Roberta Rose, and yes, I would love to go out with you."

Addiction

I remember when it had all begun
I was so very, very young
We were going to have a little fun
We did not know what we had done
I didn't know what we would do
Until someone said let's sniff some glue
After that day, when I was blue
I would hide in the corner
and huff some glue
I remember when I kicked that
I lied to myself and said, no
more, that's a fact
In college, those sleepless nights
studying for those tests
My friends gave me eight balls,
I didn't need any rest
But I kicked that too
But this time it was not easy to do
No more speed, and no more glue
But more often I was feeling blue

Then I had a wife, two kids,
and a mortgage to pay
Until my wife caught me with my
evil love one cold dark day
I lost everything, my wife, my
kids, but what can you expect
From a man with no morals or no self-respect
But my evil love has been with
me through thick and thin
She has been by my side and made
me commit so many sins
I've smoked and snorted and
stuck needles in my arm
But did not care if it did any harm
So now they will let me out today
I've done fifteen years for my crime
I will look for my evil love
Now that I have done my time
I will search for her all over town
I will search for her until she is found
Her name is
I am sure you've made your prediction
My dark evil love's name
She is called addiction

Beth

I watched as a tear rolled down her cheek,
Then I watched as it fell upon her feet.
She wraps her arms around herself in fear
Because she knows why she is here.
She's here just to get by
As she works for the next high.
Yes, she knows it will do her harm
If she keeps sticking needles in her arm.
There's not a day that goes by
That she doesn't break down and cry.
It seems so very long ago
That she went on dates to the picture show.
She has the shakes as she
waits for her next high,
Then her mind will just float
away into the sky.
She was taken advantage of, a
girl with low self-esteem;
That's why she works the streets
that are ugly and mean.
She was mistreated and shot with a gun;

That's why I'm here, her time here is done.
They call me the Grim Reaper,
or the Angel of Death.
I'm here for the girl they call Beth.
Because of her blind faith, I
give her one last thought.
With a gleam in her eye and
a smile upon her face,
She is so glad to be leaving this place.
She says, "I've been called a
hooker and a whore,
I am not either anymore."
She has faith she is ready for what is in store.
She knows her soul will be
washed pure once more.

Rose-Colored Glasses

She looks at the world
Through rose-colored glasses
As she tries to please all the masses.
The girl is so damned depressed today,
And there's nothing anyone can say.
The depression she cannot defend.
She just wants it all to end.
She looks at the world
Through rose-colored glasses
As she tries to please all the masses.
Ugly thoughts running through her head,
Lying in bed, wishing she was dead.
Then a tiny voice from outside
Brought a smile she could not hide.
It was a little boy playing with his toys
That brought her a smile and gave her joy.
She looks at the world
Through rose-colored glasses,
As she tries to please all the masses.
That's all it took to change,
And nothing will be the same.

So if you get the blues today,
Listen to what I have to say.
So if it only takes one little thing
to change your mind,
Why don't you just go out and play
and see what you can find?

Thankful

This time of year there should be a
blanket of snow on the ground.
But not this year; no snow to be found.
This time of year, we are to give thanks,
But as I grow older, my mind draws a blank.
You see, it's hard on me on this day
Because it reminds me of the
ones we lost along the way.
You see, when I remember,
it brings me to tears
To think of those we have
lost through the years.
For some, they want to run away in fear
'Cause they wonder if they
will be around next year.
There are some of us who have aged,
And when I see them, I am amazed.
I look at the picture of when I was young,
Then I look in the mirror and
see what age has done.
But for most, they seem happy and content.

They never change from event to event.
But I am thankful for my family and friends.
I will love each and every one
of them until the end.

Wasted Time

Life is like sand in an hourglass.
Rich or poor, no matter of your class,
Your time will come when you least expect it.
No matter what you do, you
won't be able to protect it.
And before it comes, you
think of wasted time;
Standing in line or waiting for
someone, that's a crime.
You see, these are stolen moments
that will never return.
You can't get them back. The minutes,
the days, the months, they are burned.
Do we start now to save those stolen
moments, or is it too late?
I know we can't make up time,
so is our past our fate?
We tend to wait for the last minute
To change our lives and everything in it.
So take your loved ones by the hand
and tell them how much you care
Because life can be cruel and truly unfair.

Humbled

Larry was sitting in a chair next to his dad's bed. He was thinking of the last few days leading up to this situation. He was remembering waiting at the Western Union place, and as always, his dad would come out with a handful of money. But this time, it seemed like a lot more.

His dad had a routine. First, he would go pay the utility bills, then go pay the landlord a couple of months back rent, and pay the next one in advance, then it was off to the grocery store for food. When he got home, he would swear he would not drink anymore. But then he would start shaking so bad he couldn't hold a cup of coffee, and he would start talking to people who weren't there. Every now and then, he would make me give him my money that I made mowing lawns and my paper route even though he would have a pocketful of money.

Then, as always, he would go to the liquor store and buy two bottles of whiskey, drink one, then be passed out by midnight.

But this time was different. We went to the liquor store first, and he bought not two bottles but a case of whiskey. On the way home, he said we would pay the bills in the morning.

That night, while he was watching TV, he could hear his dad sitting at the kitchen, drinking, yelling at people who were not there. Larry got up, turned the TV off, and went to bed.

In the morning, when Larry woke, he headed to the kitchen to make coffee. As he was passing through the living room, he saw his dad on the sofa with his back to him. He made the coffee, poured himself a cup, and sat at the kitchen table. There in front of him was a pile of money. He counted it. Seven thousand dollars. He put it in his pocket and was thinking he would let his dad sleep it off, and he would go pay bills on his own. As he was walking out the door, he paused, turned, and looked at his dad. *If I wake him, he will be in a bad mood all day. That means he will be drunk before noon and be yelling at me all day. Yes, it would be better for him to sleep it off and wake up without a hangover.* Larry turned, stepped out the door, and closed it behind him.

He went next door and paid the landlord, then he went to the back of the house, to the shed. That's where he kept his old moped. It had a hitch so he could pull his trailer with his tools and lawnmower in it. Then he headed off to pay the utility bills. After that was done, he mowed a couple of yards then delivered his papers.

He pulled the moped around to the back of the house then walked three blocks to the grocery store. By the time he got home, it was dark. He looked at the house. *Funny*, he thought, *no lights on in the house*. His dad must have gone to the bar.

He got the door open, and the stench made him gag. *The toilet must be backed up again*, he thought. He had his hands full so he couldn't turn the light on, but he could see his dad's outline in the dark. How could he sleep through that smell?

He went into the kitchen, set the bags on the table, reached over, and turned on the light. There were two empty whiskey bottles, one on the table and the other on the floor.

He headed to the bathroom. On the way, he stopped in the living room and turned on the light. The toilet was not backed up. It was his dad that stank. He must have soiled himself. There was vomit everywhere. Larry ran over to him and checked for a pulse—there was one, but weak. He ran next door to the landlords and called for an ambulance. By the time they got him to the hospital, he was brain-dead. They had him on life support the last few days, but no change. He made the decision six hours ago to unplug him. *Now here I am waiting*, and he is still breathing on his own.

Larry got up and walked over to the waiting room; he was the only one in there. Larry was so angry at his dad because he wouldn't talk about his mother. Larry didn't even know her name, didn't have a picture of her. Then he started thinking of his dad. The only advice he ever gave him didn't even make sense. He said, "Never forget who you are, and don't forget where you came from." Now that's funny. He knew who he was, a nobody, and as far back as he could remember, he has always lived in that old house.

Just then, a well-dressed man came in and sat on the sofa across Larry, looked at him, and said, "You okay?"

For some strange reason, Larry opened up to this man and said, "I never had a mom. My dad was a drunk. No relatives that I know of, no friends, and the sad thing is, I have no one to call to tell them of the bad news about my dad. I now know what it's like to be truly alone in this world."

The man just looked at him. Larry could see the tears well up in his eyes, and Larry could feel tears roll down his own cheeks. "I don't even have a picture of my mom, don't even know her name, and I don't feel any remorse for unplugging my dad. I love my dad, yet I shed no tears for him. I shed tears for me. I'm alone."

The man cleared his throat and said, "Larry, you are not alone. I am so sorry."

He reached out his hand to shake then said, "How rude of me. You don't even know who I am. My name is David Green, your uncle and your dad's brother. I have taken the liberty of giving the doctor my cell number and room number at the hotel so we can be reached anytime, anyplace. Let's go to the hotel and order room service. I have a stack of photo albums you can look through of your mom, Cindy, your dad, Mason, your grandpa Lewis, and of me, of course. After all, they're your albums."

Larry just stared at the man or, well, his uncle!

His uncle said, "Close your mouth before you catch a fly. Let's go back to our hotel. You have your own suite next to mine. I am sorry we have not been able to talk before now, but your dad had a court order stopping us from talking to you. I am sure it was the alcohol thinking for him. He blamed the company for his troubles."

David said, "Let's go."

When they got to the hotel, David ordered steaks from room service. Then he grabbed an album, opened it, and started to explain every picture—who was in it and where it was taken. He also explained when Mason and David were in high school, their dad made them work in shipping at the company. One weekend, at the beach, they met Cindy. They both dated her, but she had eyes for Mason.

"Since I was older, I went to college to learn engineering and electronics. Your dad was promoted to sales when I was away. He never went to college. When I came back, the company was in bad shape. I redesigned some old switches and got new patents. Your dad took them to the government two days before we were to let our twenty employees go and close the doors to the company for good, and just like that, we were rich and made millions on contracts. At one time, we had a hundred and fifty employees, but now our products are outdated, and we are just breaking even."

"Where is this company?" Larry asked.

David said, "In Tampa, Florida. It's the Green Specialty Switch Company. Look, it's getting late. Let's call it a night and pick this up in the morning."

David handed him a key card, "Your suite's next door."

The next morning, Larry showered, dressed, went to his uncle's room, and knocked.

"Come in," David yelled.

As Larry walked in, he saw his uncle sitting in a chair looking tired. Larry said, "Did you get any sleep last night?"

"Very little," David replied.

"I got the call on your dad about three this morning. I let you sleep because I know you have been at your dad's side the last few days and didn't sleep while you were there."

"How did you know that?" Larry said.

David said, "Well, the house you live in and the landlord's house belong to you. The rent you paid was the landlords pay to keep me informed about you and your dad. Oh yes, and he got to live there for free."

"Here," David said, "upon his death, I am to give this to you." He handed Larry an envelope.

Larry sat down and opened it. Inside were two pictures and a letter. One was a wedding picture of his mom and dad, the other was a picture of his mom in a hospital holding a baby—him, no doubt. The letter read,

Son, if you are reading this, it means I have died. I want to tell you I'm sorry about your mom. You were only a couple of weeks old when she died, and it was all my fault. I was driving that night. You see, I made her go to a company dinner for me when she wanted to stay home with you. She went anyway for me. And because of that, I could not live the good life without her. I left everything behind—the company, my brother, and dad. I am sorry I made you live with my selfish guilt and put my burden on you. A father should not make his son live through this. Your uncle David is a good man. He will take you under his wing and show you how to make it in life. I know ending it this way for you will be like walking into a dark room having to feel your way through, hoping not to bump into something or fall, but your uncle David will be there to shine a light for you, to show you the way.

I did a good thing for you. You have a lot of money in the bank, and you own three quarters of the company. Talk to David about it. And the only advice I can give you is what my dad told me. Never forget who you are and never forget where you came from. Forgive me, my son. I love you.

David watched Larry cry, then he, too, let the tears fall. When they composed themselves, David said, "Let's take care of your dad, then we will fly to Tampa. You have a decision to make. You can do one of two things. One, you can sell the patents and the company, or two, you can go to college, take engineering and business, and see if you can turn the company around. Either way, it's a win-win deal for you. But I have to warn you, if you take over the company, you will have to work hard while you're going to college. I can show you what I know."

Larry smiled at him and said, "I like a challenge." Then he said, "I know Dad wanted to be cremated. I know what to do with the ashes."

"Okay then," said David.

They were walking down the street with an urn full of Mason's ashes. David said, "Where are we going?"

Larry smiled and said, "Cooter's."

David asked, "What's a cooter?"

Larry smiled. "It's a bar."

"A bar," said David.

"Yep, a bar," said Larry.

They walked inside, and Larry asked the bartender who Cooter was. The bartender smiled. "That's me, and you're Mason's boy, Larry, right? Say, I'm sorry to hear about your dad. I have been waiting for you to show up."

"How did you know it was me?" Larry asked.

Cooter said, "You look just like him. Your dad might have drank too much, but he was a good man, and he was so proud of you." Larry's heart swelled. He and David just looked at each other.

Cooter said, "Your dad had a lot of friends here."

Larry said, "I was to bring you his ashes. You would know what to do with them."

"You bet," Cooter said. "It will be my honor. You see, years ago, I was homeless. I came in here, your dad bought me a drink. He bought me drinks all night. I told him I needed a job. He told me if I would clean myself up and sober up, he would help me get a job. So I did, and he got me a job here as a bartender. When the owner got sick and was going to sell this place, your dad got me a loan to buy this place. Whenever one of his friends died and nobody would step up to pay for a funeral, he would pay to have them cremated. He then pointed to a back wall. There were two shelves with twenty-four urns on them and one small shelf above them. He paid to have them cremated, and to pay back the loan that I had with him, every year when the date comes on each urn, I am to buy a round for the house. That's how I am to pay him back, and as long as I own this bar, I will honor the deal."

Larry never had any kind of pride for his dad until now. He was proud of his dad. He looked at David, and he could see it on his face also.

David said, "Well, shall we go to your house and pick up what you want to take with you?"

Larry said, "There is one thing I want to do before I leave." And as they were driving to the house, he told David about a kid, fifteen years old, who only had a mom, no dad. Larry would let him cut a few lawns once in a while so he could make money. He wanted to take the moped, trailer, mower, and tools and drop them off at the kid's house.

Larry said, "And we can give the landlord both houses. I won't be coming back."

David looked at Larry. "I see a lot of your dad in you, and I have to say, it was not your dad's fault that your mom died. Ironically, it was the other driver who was drunk. Your dad was sober, he walked away without a scratch. But the next day, your dad got drunk and every day after that. We had him committed twice, but each time he got out, he would drink harder. Then he took you and moved away. Well, it's in the past now. Let's not dwell on it and move on."

When they got to Tampa, Larry went to school, and David showed him all he could, but the company was still just breaking even. After three years, Larry was thinking of selling out. He talked to David about it, and David said, "Whatever you want to do, but let's wait till the end of the year. We will be giving our employees a chance to find new jobs, or take a chance and hope the new owners will keep them on."

"Okay," Larry said, "we will tell them the company will be for sale at the first of the month. If we can't sell it by the end of the year, we will close the doors."

Just before lunch, he was talking to one of the engineers in the R and D department about the springs in their switches. They needed to find a new design for their spring parts. He had the conversation stuck in his head. He said to himself, *What am I doing? I am going to sell the company.* But there it was, stuck in his head.

Larry liked to play all kinds of games and sports. He liked the challenge, and he was a competitive guy. Every day for lunch, he would go to the park a mile away and find a group who would let him play with them. He loved playing disc golf, but today he couldn't get his head into the game because of the conversation he had stuck in his mind. He watched another player throw his disc into the woods. Larry smiled to himself and was thinking, *Dumbass*, when he then did the same thing. He went to look for his disc, he found it, but as he was walking up to it, he saw it was upside down on the other player's disc. This looked like two contacts on one of their switches, but they were laying on a cushion of leaves. *That's it!* he said to himself. He grabbed his disc, went and jumped in his car, and made it to the company in record time. He went looking for the engineer he was talking to earlier, found him, and said, "Memory foam." They put a switch together with the foam. It worked. They applied for a patent and got it.

Larry put a bid on a government contract and got it. He got not just one, but dozens. In less than a year, they made billions—not millions, but billions.

His uncle David retired, and Larry ran the company by himself. He expanded by buying other companies that made other products. One company he owned was a computer design company. They made games for online playing. He loved playing the games.

He didn't want to let anyone know who he was, so he gave himself a game name. His tag was Wicked Warrior. From time to time he would notice a player tagged Live Wire. He was good. Larry would find himself looking for Live Wire to play. They would take turns challenging each other to different games. One day, he asked Live Wire if he was set up for audio chat. Live Wire said yes. That changed the game because they started talking smack to each other while playing.

One day, Live Wire said he didn't feel like playing, but he wanted to chat. He knew of a chat room they could go to and talk. Larry said okay. Live Wire told him where to go, so they went.

Larry said, "I like playing these games. Makes me feel like a kid again. How old are you?"

"Twenty-two," said Live Wire. "How old are you?"

"Thirty-five," said Larry.

Live Wire said he was from a little town outside Oklahoma City and was on his own now. He said his dad liked to get drunk and slap him around and was in prison doing life now, so he went to live with his uncle, and he was a drunk also and liked to slap him around. "But I try to find good in everybody. They both gave me good advices."

"And what was that?" Larry asked.

"Well, my dad told me to never forget who you are and where you came from," said Live Wire. Then he said, "You can call me Sam or Sammy. All my friends do."

Larry said, "Well, I got the same advice from my dad and uncle too."

That's when Sam cut him off. Larry heard a big roar from Sam's end and heard a scream. Then Sam's end went dead. Larry said, "Hey, man, you there?" He heard nothing. *Well at least I have an online friend*, he thought. He was a hard worker; never had time to make friends.

The next day, no Sam, nor the next week. Four weeks went by, but it didn't matter. He hardly had time for games anymore. He had tax problems, so he started creating and hosting charities, all kinds of them—homeless, heart, liver, cancer, you name it. He would rather give to people who needed money than give it to the IRS. There was this one charity he had been working on for the last couple of weeks. It was a marathon in North Carolina called *A Run for Life* to benefit the homeless. To promote it, he put ads in the newspaper, even did a TV spot.

Larry had been working hard. He decided he needed a break, so he thought he would check out some new games one of his companies had designed. He checked out some kids' games. He was thinking these were good games for kids. He moved on to the new adult games, mostly war games.

Larry was playing a game when he heard a voice over his headset say, "You play like crap."

He was not sure, but he said, "Sam?"

"Yep," said Sam. "I challenge you to this game."

Larry beat him. Larry said, "I challenge you to this other game."

Sam had beat Larry five games in a row. "Sam, where have you been?" said Larry.

Sam said, "I told you I work for the government. They sent me to a place where there were no cell or internet services. I challenge you to a game called *A Run for Freedom*."

Larry knew this game and liked it because he was good at it. It was a POW game where you escape a POW camp and fight your way to freedom. You pick up weapons, equipment, and food along the way. His company sold a different version to the government for training our troops. "Let's play," said Larry.

Sam said, "I never turn down a challenge. Let's play."

From the start, they needled each other, talking smack. Sam beat him six games in a row.

"Had enough," said Sam.

Larry hated to lose. He was really pissed off. He wanted to beat this guy so bad. He said, "Let's do something real. I challenge you to a run. I will pay for your transportation to and from and your hotel room." There was silence in his headphones.

"Are you afraid I will meet some fat, geeky-looking guy who can't run?" Still no comeback.

"What's wrong? Cat got your tongue? I bet a steak dinner."

Sam finally spoke, "You must be talking about the North Carolina Run. I will pay for my own room and transportation, I take no handouts. I will see you at the starting line, Mr. Larry Green."

"Wait," said Larry, "how did you know my name?"

Sam said, "Man, you are so stupid. If you look at the top of your page, you will notice your company logo with your picture beside it. You have ads in the newspaper and on TV, and there were a few times you told me of games that were coming that weren't online yet. So there's only one way you would have that information. Aren't you getting a little old to be running with young guys? What's the matter? Cat got your tongue? Challenge accepted, Mr. Larry Green." Then Sam broke the connection.

Larry just sat there, mouth open, looking at his logo with his picture beside it, thinking he was not sure whether to be mad or happy that his friend was back. Well, friend online anyway. It occurred to him that he didn't know what Sam looked like or that he didn't know Sam's last name. He looked at the logo once more and was thinking, *I am stupid. Wicked Warrior my ass*, and started laughing.

Larry was walking up and down the starting line, trying to figure out which one of these guys were Sam. When the race started, Larry had no idea how out of shape he was. There were hills he had to run up and down. Two miles from the finish line, three or four people fell in front of Larry. He jumped over them but went down himself. He scraped his elbows and knees, and it hurt.

While he was on the ground, a hand appeared in front of him to help him up, but Larry was not looking at the hand; he was looking past the hand at two running shoes with what looked like poles sticking out of them, which had drops of blood on them. They ran up to just below his knees. Larry grabbed the hand and got up.

The young man with the prosthetics asked, "Are you okay? You went down pretty hard."

Larry's reply was, "I am all right."

"Good," said the young man, then turned, and ran off.

When Larry reached the finish line, the young man with the prosthetics came over to him, reached out his hand. As they were shaking hands, he said, "Sergeant Samuel Martinez, Mr. Green. I think you owe me a steak dinner." Larry, with his mouth opened, just stared at Sam.

Larry then said, "Won't they give you a wheelchair?"

Sam said, "Oh, they did. Three of them, but I gave them to guys who needed them more than me, and I told them I wanted legs. They gave me these and told me I was not healed yet and not to run on them yet. But I never turn down a challenge."

Larry said, "I am sorry. I didn't know," then just stared at Sam once more with his mouth open.

Sam just smiled and said, "How could you know? And close your mouth before you catch a fly."

Sam said, "The day we got cut off, we went under a mortar attack. My tent took the first round, it took my legs. Then there was this guy, didn't really know him, but we played cards together. I poked fun at him all the time because he had a lisp. This guy took a belly wound, he was bleeding bad. His name was Frank. He tied off my legs to stop the blood flow and piggybacked me to safety. He didn't care for himself, he cared for me. A few minutes after he got me to the medics, he died. I have never been so humbled in my life." Sam had tears well up in his eyes.

Larry wiped away his tears and said, "You made me remember something."

"What's that?" Sam said.

"Advice, that's what. My dad told me never forget who you are or where you come from," said Larry. "I stand in front of you humbled, and I want to do something for you. I would like to make you a partner in my company."

Sam said, "Hey, I don't take handouts."

Larry said, "I'm sure you don't. That's why you will start in shipping and work your way up. I think I owe you a steak dinner. You hungry? And while we are eating, you can tell me everything you know about switches."

My Last Prayer

Here I lay in my hospital bed
A freight train running through my head

Things are not so clear
For I know not why I am here

My eyes are half open, and I can hear
With needles, tubes, and a machine
giving me life, it would appear

He will not make it through the
night, doctors tell my family and
Friends
Am I to believe that this is the end

O Lord, I will not lie, I believe in
you, but with some doubt
Are you real, well, I shall soon find out

I question will there be a blinding light
Or singing angels that are in flight

So many questions, it's the answers that I fear
I feel myself fading, this much is clear

So upon my last night, I will
tell you my last prayer
Lord, it's simple, not complicated
with so many layers

This is my prayer

Lord, help my family and friends
love you and know what you're
About
Just so when their time comes,
there will be no doubt

Prayer

It was a cold and rainy day
When I slid off the road
With that load of hay
If you live your life without sin
He will watch over you
You can depend
The wreck happened so very fast
They say that day should have been my last
It's true I should have not walked away
Believe in him is all I can say
If this should ever happen to you
Remember he gave his life for you
So every night before you sleep
Pray to him your soul to keep
Then maybe one day
You may walk away
For prayer is a small price to pay

Reincarnation

The crying and the sorrow fade away
When I awake, will it be a new day?
It is dark, then there is light
That's funny, I feel I am in flight
I think I was on my way home
Now my wife will live life all alone
They say my belief should guide me
But shouldn't the Lord be beside me?
I hope to raise into the light
Whatever happens, I shall not fight
I feel like a moth pulled to a flame
There is no wrong, no one to blame
Look, what do I see?
It's a new life waiting for me

Time to Move On

Well, I'm sitting here all alone
In our little place we call home.
It seems like just yesterday
Since cancer took you away.
And I don't know what to do,
Living my life without you.
Life's just not the same.
There's no one to blame.
Well, baby, sure miss your smile;
It's been gone a long while.
I have shed all these tears.
How do I move on from here?
It's not the loneliness that appears;
It's living without you that I fear.
Yesterday has come and gone.
People tell me I must move on.
Please forgive me if I find someone new,
But I need help to get rid of the blues.
I don't want a heart that's dark and cold,
So send me a sign to move
on, if I may be so bold.

There You Are

Malachi, Josh, and Donna grew up together. Now fresh out of high school, they were going to enjoy the summer before thinking about college.

That summer, Malachi discovered the Lord. And Josh and Donna? Well, they discovered each other. It's funny, you can be friends with someone for years, and somewhere along the way, you cross the line, and you realize that a friend means more to you than just a friend. Before the end of summer, they both got jobs and moved in together. They were enjoying life.

Malachi was enjoying the church. For him, the church would be his life. He became Josh and Donna's spiritual leader and, in a very short time, became a minister.

When Josh and Donna got married, their friend and spiritual leader, Malachi, performed the ceremony.

Malachi encouraged them to be more involved with the church, so that's how they ended up at the lake that day. The church had a weekend retreat every third week of the month—a Friday, Saturday, and Sunday.

Josh and Donna were not sure if they would attend because Donna was seven and a half months along with their first child and not feeling well. But they went anyway.

Friday night, it sprinkled all night. Saturday was light rain. Around noon, they all got together to pray the rain would stop, and it did not; it came down harder. So the decision was made to break camp.

Josh had Donna sit in the car while he and Malachi went around and helped everyone pack and load their cars in the pouring rain.

They had only gotten a mile, at the T, where they would make a right turn to head toward town, when their world turned literally upside down.

Josh thought a bug was crawling up his face. He swatted at it. He opened his eyes and looked at his hand. There was blood. The blood was from the corner of his mouth. He was upside down, hanging by the seat belt.

He hurt everywhere. He heard a moan. It was coming from him. He looked over to Donna, but she was not there. He looked around, but no Donna. He reached in his pocket and got his knife out, cut the seat belt, and crawled out of what was left of their car.

He lay on the cold, wet road and looked at the devastated trees, stripped of branches and tops. High-lines were down. Part of a roof to a house was lying in the road. A tornado, no doubt.

He looked over to his right, and lying next to a bathtub was Donna. He lay there and could not move. He said out loud, "Please, God. Give me strength." It took a few minutes to get to his feet, but he made it. He felt numb, but he stumbled over to Donna. He called out her name, but she did not move. He felt for a pulse, and with relief, he felt one. Somehow he felt the strength come to him as he picked Donna up in his arms, turned, and started to walk to town.

The next thing he knew, he was lying on the gurney in an emergency room with a doctor standing next to him, holding three pieces of paper, looking a little pissed, saying, "Will you please sign these so we can do the surgeries?"

"You want me to sign those?" said Josh.

"Yes," said the doctor. "The first is so we can fix both of your hips, your leg, and all of your ribs.

You did damage to your liver. One of your lungs will have to be taken out, and you ripped a hole in your heart. You may never walk again. The second paper is so we can do a C-section to save the baby; and the third, I'm sorry, but it's to leave your wife on life support or take her off. She has no brain activity."

"Is Malachi here? I need to consult with my spiritual leader before I make my decision."

The doctor said, "He was here before you were. I will send him in. But we need to act fast. You are running out of time."

Malachi came into the room and ran over to Josh and grabbed his hand. Josh had never before seen Malachi like this. He was crying, shaking, and so upset. Josh said, "I have known you since we were two years old, and never once have I seen you cry."

Malachi said, "Man, I am truly afraid of losing you or, well, all three of you. All of you are my family. The ambulance driver said he found you two miles away from your car where the tornado dropped you."

Josh smiled and said, "No, God gave me the strength to carry Donna before I passed out. It's just like you said, if you believe, then anything is possible. So let's pray, then I'll sign those papers. Calm down. Everything will work itself out one way or another."

Josh prayed, "Please, God. If you can find it in your heart to let Donna and our child live and take me in their place, I shall be your servant for eternity." That's when Josh passed out.

Josh heard whispering long before he opened his eyes. It was Malachi, head bowed, holding the Bible with both hands, praying. Josh said, "I'll sign those papers now."

Malachi said, "It's already been done. Everything's been taken care of."

"Wait, wait, wait. What do you mean everything's been taken care of?" Josh cried.

Malachi said, "Three weeks ago, I signed the papers. Your baby girl will be here another two weeks before they release her. We buried Donna two weeks ago. They didn't know if you would recover. So let's pray for your daughter and your recovery."

Josh was mad. He said, "No, I will never pray again. I believed, by the grace of God, Donna would live. But instead I am a cripple, and I will have to raise my daughter alone."

Malachi said, "Please don't lose your faith in God. I will help raise your daughter."

Josh said, "Too late. I lost my faith when my wife died."

Malachi said, "Josh, she never made it to the hospital, my friend. The only reason she was on life support was to keep your child alive. I love all three of you, man. You are my family. You are my brother, and Donna was like a sister. And your little girl, I would be proud to call her my niece. Look, I didn't think you would want Donna just to stay like that. So I was the one who signed for you, your daughter, and Donna. So let's pray."

Josh said, "No no no. I'm trying not to be mad right now, okay? I don't want religion in my life right now. I believed because of you, and I believed all my life. When I needed it most, it failed me."

Malachi said, "It's a miracle you two are alive. If it—"

"No," said Josh, "I don't need a sermon or any religion in my life right now. I love you like a brother, and you did the right thing. I thank you for stepping in and taking care of everything."

He could see the hurt leave Malachi's face and said, "I need to give my daughter a name, and I have a perfect name. Cierra Nicole. And please respect my wish not to push religion on her. She will have free will. If she wants religion, she will find it on her own, not from me or you. I shall not deny her that right."

Malachi said, "I shall respect your wish." And true to his word, he didn't push religion on Cierra.

It took almost three years, with the help of therapy, braces, and walkers, for Josh to walk again, and he still had to use a cane. He was proud of two things: one, that he would walk when they told him he would never walk again, and two, he was the only person to call his daughter Cee.

She looked so much like Donna, with honey-blond hair and blue eyes; and when she was confused, one side of her mouth would go up into a half grin, and at the corner of her mouth was a dimple. Donna would be so proud.

When she was ten, Josh took her to the mall to look for shoes that she could run in for track. As they walked in the entrance to the mall, a map was hanging on the wall. She was looking for a shoe store when Josh said, "Do you see it on the map, but you aren't sure where it's at? Just remember this, wherever you go, there you are."

Cee just looked at him and started laughing. From then on, it was their inside joke.

It was also the day she asked if she could go to Malachi's church. She said her friends went there. She said she asked Malachi, and he said she needed to talk to her dad about it. Cee said Uncle Malachi looked sad when he said it.

Josh thought, *He is staying true to his word.* (And he was.) *He helped teach her about jogging, riding a bike, hunting and fishing, and softball. We both did.*

Now at sixteen, she was going to church regularly and I had discovered reincarnation. I liked the concept, and if you are supposed to believe in something, why not this?

Cee came home one day and said, "Dad, we have a game on Friday at one o'clock. The schedule is messed up, so I don't know where."

Josh said, "Well, there you go. Just remember, wherever you go, there you are."

Cee just looked at him and said, "Daddy!" Then she started laughing. She hadn't called him daddy in a long time. It brought tears to his eyes. She said as soon as the coach calls her, she would tell him where to go.

Josh said, "I will change my doctor's appointment."

Cee said, "No no. Uncle Malachi will take me. We talked to the coach, he said it was okay. You go to the doctor's and then come to the game."

"Okay," said Josh. He was thinking to himself, *I really need to see the doctor.* He had been getting dizzy and feeling tired lately.

When Friday arrived, he wasn't feeling well at all. He got up late, too late to fix Cee breakfast. He heard her in the kitchen. By the time he was up, she had already left. He didn't get to say I love you or say goodbye. They did it every day.

He felt this was not going to be a good day at all. He was almost late for his appointment. Josh wished he hadn't gone at all. It was very bad news. It was his heart. When he was in the tornado, the rip he got in his heart was at a valve. The tissue around the valve was dying, so no bypass; and because he only had one lung and liver damage, no transplant. The doctor told him he may have one to two years and will be very lucky to make two.

He was heading to Cee's softball game. How was he going to tell Cee and Malachi? He was crying. He was wiping the tears with the sleeve of his shirt when he drifted across the center line and hit the dump truck head-on.

Josh was lying on a gurney in a room with Cee, Malachi, and a doctor. His eyes were closed, but he could see them. How could this be? He could also hear them. Cee was crying. Josh was telling her not to cry, but she could not hear him.

Malachi asked, "Did he suffer?"

The doctor said, "No. The death was instantaneous. There was no pain." He asked the doctor if he would like to join them while they prayed.

Josh was thinking, *Man, Malachi, you never give up, do you?* That's when he heard it, the sweetest voice he ever heard. It was Donna's voice. It said, "It's time, my love."

Josh said, "Time for what?"

The reply was, "Time to go."

He said, "Where are you? And go where?" He didn't remember standing up, but he was upright, not standing, floating. He wanted to know where Donna was, but all of a sudden, he was in a tunnel of light, or more like a beam of light, and it was so bright and blinding he felt like he was flying. How long has he been doing this? It felt like a second, or maybe eternity. Somehow he knew time did not matter.

At some point, he had stopped in a sea of white and total silence, and the silence was deafening. He yelled, "Is there anyone out there?" That's when he saw his Uncle Oscar walking up to him, no, floating. Oscar was smiling, as he always did.

Josh asked, "Are we in heaven?"

Oscar said, "No, we are in the waiting room." He said this without moving his lips, but Josh heard every word.

"Well, some call this heaven, but others call"—pointing down—"that heaven. Have you not heard the phrase 'heaven on earth'?"

"But I—"

Oscar cut him off, "Don't believe everything you read."

Josh saw a lady he knew that died a couple of years ago but couldn't remember her name. He went to wave when he noticed he was wearing his favorite suit. He looked at his uncle; he was wearing an OU ball cap, a Sooner T-shirt, and blue jeans—that's what he was buried in.

"Oh, Donna told me to tell you she always loved you," Josh said. "Where is she?"

"She was called back."

"Called back?" Josh said.

Oscar said, "Yes. So will you."

"How long will that be?"

"Don't know," Oscar said. "At some point in time, your questions will all be answered, but it won't do you any good."

"Why?" said Josh.

"Because when you go back, you will do it with a clean slate. They will wipe your memory clean. That way, you will have free will to decide what you want to believe in. You will get to experience pain, sorrow, happiness, love, confusion, and so much more. You will experience life all over again. And at some point, you will have every question you ever had answered, even the meaning of life, but it won't do you any good because it will be wiped clean."

Oscar said, "All that matters is you believe in something. If you don't believe in anything, you stay down there as a spirit or ghost until you believe. You see, if you believe in something like God, then you live your life a certain way. If you believe in reincarnation, then you live differently. You see, everyone is the same but all different. You make a full circle. If you are down there and don't believe, then you are dazed and confused. You block the flow, no full circle. But if you believe, you have purpose, you have a direction, you see.

"There is no right way or wrong way as long as you believe everything will be fine," Oscar said. "Got to go. I feel the pull of the light."

"When will I go?"

"When they have a spot for you."

Josh yelled as Oscar was floating away, "Is there a god?"

"All your questions will be answered," said Oscar.

Josh saw someone he was sure he knew. The man turned to look at Josh then came to him.

Josh said, "I've met you before, I'm sure of it." Josh heard a laugh in his mind.

"Yes, you have. A few lives ago, you were my dad. Then the last time we met, you were my pet dog, Mongo."

Josh said, "Somehow I remember that."

The man said, "Just call me Mason. It makes it easy, and I will be happy to tell you some things, like this whole concept. We will start here. You leave here to be reborn. When you are reborn, you have a purpose. That's to help a person believe in something. You see, you don't do it by yourself. Once you serve your purpose, you earn your ticket. It gets you back here to start all over again, full circle.

"It's not as easy as it sounds. When you hear your 'number' has been called, that means you may have to get a certain number to believe before you earn your ticket to get back here. Your last 'ticket,' even though you didn't believe in God, you gave your life so Cierra would believe. Your death sealed the deal. That's when you made the 'Turn.' The turn is when you become a spirit as you are now. What I see of you is the image that you reflect in your past life. Watch." Mason took his arm and passed through

Josh. "You are just a spirit until you make the 'turn.' The turn is when you become a living being or when you become a spirit. You may be a tree or dog or man or woman, any living being. Just by believing, you support our existence. And don't worry about if you become a ghost. We both have been there. It's simple. Just believe you earned your ticket. And don't worry if you become an animal or a tree. Your image only reflects the last person you were."

Mason said, "We will see each other again. I feel the pull of the light. Just remember, it's all complicated, but you will understand before your memory will be wiped clean. A clean slate for a full circle."

Josh had a moment of clarity when he got all his answers and understood all, but he did not lose his memory; it did not fade. At first, Josh could not tell what they were talking about, but he did know the voices. It was Cee and Malachi.

Malachi said, "Raymond Lewis is a fine name. Your dad and Gene would be proud."

Cee said, "Dad, yes. Gene, not sure."

Malachi said, "Gene would have been proud, I am sure. He loved you, Cierra."

Cierra said, "No, he didn't. I knew six months after we got married, it was a mistake. He was running around on me from the beginning. All he wanted from me was to help spend Dad's insurance money. That's how he got the hot rod he killed himself in and that teenage girl he was with. Dad would have never approved of Gene. Gene's been gone seven months now, and his parents are still trying to sue me. Can't blame them, not after finding a beer and a motel key in the car. Dad always told me the world can be a cold, cruel place, but sometimes things have a way of working themselves out. You just have to believe."

Malachi said, "Let me hold him. I will take Ray for a walk. You get some sleep. You looked tired."

Cierra said, "Okay. I feel tired. I think I can sleep for a week. After your walk, take him to the nursery. They will take care of him there."

Malachi was walking down the hallway. Josh was trying to say something, but all he could get out was "Goo" and "Gaa." He felt a tickle in his throat. He cleared it and spit.

Malachi entered the lounge and sat down. No one else was in the room. He looked at the baby and said, "Well, little man, I will be the first to pray for you."

Josh said, "Malachi, you never give up, do you?"

Well, Malachi almost threw the baby but just held him out arms' length and stared at Raymond. He said, "Ray-Ray, did you say that?"

Josh said, "Ray-Ray. Come on. Really?" That's when Josh's memory went blank. Then all he could do is do what babies do. He closed his eyes, started to drift off to sleep while filling his diaper. Josh was gone.

Malachi was staring at the baby, and Raymond was asleep. Malachi was thinking, *I miss Josh so much. I only imagined his voice, that's got to be it.* He stood up and said, "Okay, let's not pray right now. Let's get you back to the nursery."

Once when Ray was twelve, before school, he asked Cierra if he could go to the park after school to play catch with his friend Mark. He said he wanted to break in his new baseball glove. The park was only four blocks away from the house.

Cierra said, "I'll pick you up at four-thirty. Be ready to go home, okay?"

Ray said, "Sure, Mom."

When Cierra got to the park, he was waiting for her. He ran as he was getting into the car. Cierra said, "Where's your glove?"

Ray looked puzzled. "Oh yeah, I know where it is." He got out of the car and ran across the park. He was gone for thirty minutes.

She said, "That boy!"

She got out, looked around, but didn't see him. So she got back in, started the car, and drove to the other side of the park. She saw him and honked the horn. He came running over with the glove in his hand.

She said, "Where did you go?"

Ray said, "Well, I found my glove and got turned around. Couldn't remember where you parked."

Cierra smiled and said, "Just remember, wherever you go, there you are."

Ray looked at her, blinked, and said, "Mom," then started a big ole belly laugh.

It brought tears to her eyes and a big smile on her face that she had for days. And now, that was their inside joke, the one she and her dad had.

Then one day that started like any other day, she got dazed and confused and scared until she remembered what her dad told her. The world can be a cold and cruel place, but if you believe, things will work themselves out.

Ray was seventeen. He called Cierra at work and said, "Mark and I want to load our dirt bikes in Mark's truck and go to the lake to ride the trails. I know we always go with Uncle Malachi, but he has things to do. It will only be for three or four hours."

Cierra said, "Okay, but be home before dark and wear a helmet."

Ray said, "All right. Be home before dark, and I will wear a helmet. Malachi always says wear a skid lid, whatever that means."

Before Ray hung up, he said, "Love you, Mom. Bye."

Cierra froze. He always says "Love you, Mom," but never "Bye." It sent a chill up Cierra's back.

Two hours later, she got the call. Mark said, "Ray hit a tree. He split his helmet into two pieces. We called 9-1-1."

Cierra said, "Where are you at?"

Mark said, "We are parked at the boat ramp, but we are on the other side of the docks."

Cierra jumped in her car and raced to the lake. When she got there, on the other side of the docks, no boys or dirt bikes, so she drove over to the boat ramp. She saw Mark's red truck, but again, no boys or dirt bikes. She called Mark's cell, no answer. She tried again, still no answer. So she called Ray's cell—no answer. She kept trying a dozen times before Mark answered.

Cierra said, "Where are you?"

Mark said, "The ambulance came and picked us up. We are at the hospital."

She was frantic now. She was halfway to town before she remembered to call Malachi.

When she got to the emergency room that she knew so well, the doctor was waiting on her.

"How is he?" she asked.

The doctor told her it was not good, to brace herself. "His brain is swelling. If we don't relieve the pressure, he will die, and as it stands now, he most likely will have brain damage. We need to wait a couple of hours. If the swelling doesn't go down, we will drill holes in his skull to relieve pressure. We are doing some tests on him, so it will be a while before you can go in. Go get some coffee or make calls if you need to, and as soon as we are done with the tests, you can go in, okay?"

Cierra said, "Do you know Malachi?"

The doctor said, "Yes."

"Will you send him up to the chapel upstairs?"

The doctor said, "He is walking in the doors right now."

She ran to him and hugged him. "How bad is it?"

"Let's go upstairs to the chapel and pray. I will explain on the way."

When they got to the chapel, Malachi's tears were flowing freely. Cierra could see Malachi was in a state of confusion.

She said, "Malachi, when we lost Dad, you were there to fill his shoes. I looked to you like you were my dad. You have been my pillar of strength. Don't lose your faith now. I look to you for that. This whole town looks up to you. Dad lost his belief, but he was always there to guide me down the right path. When I lost him, you were there to take his place. I need you now. Ray needs your prayers. Like my dad said, 'It will work itself out one way or the other, then life goes on.' Will you be okay?"

Malachi said, "Yes, I will. You go down and check on Ray while I compose myself," as he was wiping the tears away. "I will be down shortly."

The doctor was standing outside of Ray's room. "Well, the swelling has stopped. He's not out of the woods yet, but it's looking better. You can go in and sit with him if you like."

Cierra went in, pulled a chair up to the side of his bed. She knew that her dad and Gene had all been in this room. She wondered if her mom was here also. She bent her head forward to pray, then she froze when she heard her dad's voice. "I got to meet my grandson. I don't know how, but we talked in spirit only. He told me he needed to tell you he loves you and wanted to say goodbye, but I knew it was me who needed to tell you that. Also, always believe, that's what matters. Remember that, if nothing else. Remember that. Then you will make a full circle."

Josh said, "I feel myself fading. I need to say I love you, Cee, and everything will be all right. I got to go, and wherever you go, there you are."

Cee was crying and smiling at the same time. She said, "I miss and love you, Daddy."

This brought so much joy to Josh as he faded away and let Ray take over.

Ray looked at his mom and said, "Did you just call me Daddy? Wow, I feel like I was in a dream. I never met Grandpa, but I feel like he has been with me all my life. It's like he whispered in my ear what you always tell me."

Cierra and Ray looked in each other's eyes and at the same time said, "Just remember, wherever you go, there you are."

Fortitude

The winter season is coming around
As he watches the leaves fall onto the ground.
It's bitter and cold as the day turns to night,
But still, no blanket of white.
He thinks of all the people
he said bad things to,
And he wonders why he sits in solitude.
He feels the loneliness fill the room.
He wishes he could sweep it
away with a broom.
Time to change and show a little fortitude
And have a change in his attitude.
He has an idea as a smile
creeps upon his face.
He should buy gifts and decorate this place.
After all, it's Christmastime.
He will invite everyone over
to have a little fun.
He will tell them he loves them and
sorry for what he has done.

He grabs his hat and coat and opens
the door as he steps into the night,
Then he stops and smiles as he
sees a blanket of white.

Friends

There are people who claim
to be your friends,
But will these people be around in the end?
Your true friends defend you
when you're not around.
When whispers start, these other
so-called friends cannot be found.
Some people say they have
friends from coast to coast,
But will these friends be around
when you need them the most?
Are these people there to tear
down the things that you do?
Or are they there to help with your problem
to make sure you make it through?
So when I am in trouble and I am in need,
I call my friend to answer my pleas.
You see, my friends really
don't need to be asked.
They just do; that's what
makes a friendship last.

So when I am with my family and friends,
My love for them comes from the heart.
You see, my family and friends,
Well, it's hard to tell them apart.

Carole's Friend

You think I don't love you.
You think I don't care.
I really need to tell you,
I love the time we share.
But there are times I wonder
If you even care.
It's us together. Man, what a pair.
A couple of things you need to hear,
Like when we sit down to dinner
And all that you do is stare.
What about that stinky breath
And that nasty, dirty hair
And those daily walks
With one-sided conversations?
Boy, if you could talk,
Wouldn't you be a sensation.
You wonder who I'm talking about.
Well, let me tell you, my friends.
It's my dog, Rosco, and he is my best friend.

Old

You cry and you whine about growing old.
Well, let me tell you something,
if I may be so bold.
You go through life and wonder,
"How did I get this far
With scratches and bruises
and, yes, even scars?"
There are those who leave us
when they are so young.
Their lives have not even
started; they hadn't begun.
So be happy that you and the ones that
you care for have made another day.
Tell them you love them and
mean every word you say.
Because some people run
through life in a hurry,
So growing old is the least of your worries.
So take the time you can cherish,
So you can grow old before you perish.

The Simple Things

There are times when I wonder why
People sometimes let the simple things go by.
They think these things will always be there,
And when they're not, they
cry and say it's not fair.
For example, life is a simple thing,
But people make it difficult.
Wait, let me explain.
You see, life is what you make it.
You don't have to inject drama and fake it.
But long ago, we mixed religion and politics.
Now our world is filled with
chaos and cannot be fixed.
To make a point, people want
to get in your face.
I want to tell them, we're all the
same; we're the human race.
That's why we should experience
the simple things
And live life and see what it brings.

Time to Live

Well, I'm living on borrowed time.
If I don't live it, it would be a crime.
I really don't know what to do
But share all my time with you.
I remember when I first saw you,
I was looking at the morning dew.
Then I saw you on your morning run
Way before the morning sun.
Well, it seemed like eternity.
I was looking for a little fun,
Then I saw your blue eyes,
then I was stunned.
You made the meaning of life more to me
Than just borrowed time, I
hope you would agree.
Was it right to pull you into my world?
Yes, I'm selfish. I made you my girl.
Well, my end could come at any time.
Until it comes, we'll be just fine.

Charlie's Legacy

Jimmie Dean sat on his horse and was looking down at the tracks. He was glad it had rained the night before; sure made it easy to track. The tracks had brought him to the mouth of this box canyon. He has been trailing four horses for two days. On these horses were bandits who robbed a stagecoach, and it was his job to catch them.

That's why he wore the tin star. He was a man with no fear. He fought in the civil war. He rode with the Pony Express, and later in life, he would become a lawyer, then a judge, even make a run for congress and even president.

He checked his pair of six-shooters with the pearl handles and made sure they were loaded and not cocked. He looked around. Tracks going into the canyon, none exiting the box canyon. He knew this area, not so much this canyon, but he liked the area.

He got off his horse and led him. The tracks went off to the right. He was thinking to himself, *Why would they come this way? Nothing this way but a rock wall.* That's when he saw it. *I'll be damned,* he said to himself. You can see the opening in the rock wall going out, not coming in. It's big enough to get a horse through the passage.

He followed it. At the end, it opened onto a ledge. Looking to the right, he could see the opening to this canyon; looking to the left, the ledge descends to the canyon floor. He looked back to the right, to the canyon opening, and on the horizon, he could see four specks moving fast. He could tell he was a full day behind.

He leaned on a giant boulder next to the passage that brought him here. He pulled off his hat and wiped his forehead with the sleeve of his shirt. He said out loud, "Never catch them standing here." He put his hat back on his head then turned left when a gleam of light almost blinded him. It took a moment for his eyes to adjust.

He reached out and touched the boulder he had been leaning on, blinked, then rubbed his eyes. Once more, he reached out and touched it. He couldn't believe his eyes. This wasn't . . . No, it couldn't be, but there it is. The boulder was not a rock, it was gold, maybe fifty times larger than his outhouse.

He placed his hand on it and smiled!

A Hundred and Fifty Years Later

JD was throwing firewood into the fireplace when his uncle Charlie came into the room.

"Good morning," he said.

Charlie said, "Boy, we need to talk."

JD said, "Oh no. What did I do now?"

Charlie smiled and said, "We need to talk about family."

JD looked a little puzzled and said, "It's just you and me."

"Yep," said Charlie, "that's what we need to talk about." Charlie sat in a chair across JD and said, "You have never been out of this state. It's time for you to explore America. Go sow your wild oats. Go explore places you would like to see. I am sure at some point nature will take its own course, and you will find a girl you would like to spend the rest of your life with, or not. You need to get out there and find out who you are, what you want to do in life. No matter if it's just to see other places or more schoolen', it's up to you.

"Anyway, you go out, and if you find some little gal to settle down with, start you a home, or you will always have this place to come back to, it's up to you."

JD said, "But where am I going to get the money? Or how am I going to go with no car?"

Charlie said, "Leave that up to me. In the meantime, start thinking about where you want to go first. Just remember one thing, you can never sell this place, it's for you to pass on to your son. When you get somewhere you will stay at for a while, call or write me. I will send more money if you need it."

JD said, "Where are we going to get the money?"

Charlie said, "Don't worry about money. The money may not last a lifetime, but this land will be here forever." The talk of money interested JD. See, he knew people in town called his uncle Charlie, "Crazy Charlie." They said he might have millions stashed away.

JD said, "I know you have money. How much you got?"

Charlie said, "The money's not important, and one day you will know. What is important is, you keep this land, and if I write you, you keep every letter. Promise me that, okay?"

JD just shook his head up and down and was thinking how they could have money. As far as he could see, all they had was this old log home on this land and an old pickup. But his uncle Charlie would always give a task like feed the livestock or mend a fence or clean the barn. And Uncle Charlie would give him more money than he needed, and he put the rest in the bank. He almost had enough to buy a nice car.

Charlie said, "JD, are you listening to me?" JD just nodded his head.

Charlie said, "It's our job to take care of it, keep it in the family. This land was given to your great-great-great-grandpa from the State for his service to the state and to his country. All the men in our family served in all the wars and conflicts all around the world. When I write you, I will tell you all I know about them, and some of it will be in their own handwriting. That's why it is important to save every one of those letters, okay?"

"Okay, I'll save every one," said JD.

A week has gone by, and JD still didn't know where he wanted to start his adventure. As he pulled the pickup into the yard, he saw a motorcycle, black and chrome, with a sidecar. Better yet, it was a Harley. He jumped out of the truck, saw his uncle Charlie standing on the porch, and said, "Nice bike. Whose is it?"

Charlie smiled and said, "Yours, dummy."

JD said, "Wow!"

They both looked the bike over then went into the house. Once in, JD saw a set of keys and a large stack of money. He had never seen that much money in one place before.

Charlie looked at him and said, "Twenty grand, don't go crazy with it. Remember, money don't make the man, man has to make the money. If you use it as you need it, it should last awhile. And when you need more, just call or write, and I will deposit it in your account. I brought this home so you could see what twenty grand in cash looked like, so you get a couple hundred out then put the rest in your account so you can have it anytime you want."

JD looked at his uncle Charlie and said, "So when do you want me to go?"

Charlie looked at JD and said, "You can go whenever you want. It doesn't have to be now or next week. I think you need to discover America and to discover who JD is. There is a lot out there for you to understand. I will send you letters—they will tell you about the men in our family, some in their own handwriting. I know you don't understand now but you will later. I want you to have a legacy to pass on to your family. I made a promise to myself that since my brother's not here, I would make sure his son would have a legacy to pass on to his family."

JD took off the next year and enjoyed himself. He had a good time and did meet that girl and got married. He put a down payment on a house on the beach in the Sunshine State. He went back to school, got himself a good job, and was doing well, thanks to Uncle Charlie.

Five years later, life was good. He had two sons with twins on the way. His uncle Charlie sent those letters every week, at times as many as ten, and also talked to him a couple of times a week on the phone. So when the phone rang that night, JD somehow knew it was his uncle Charlie.

He said, "What's up?"

Charlie said, "Well, I need you to take some time and come out and see me. I want to put the land and house in your name, so you will need to sign some papers. Oh yes, bring the letters with you. You still have them, don't you?"

JD said, "Every one of them. Is there something wrong?"

Charlie said, "No, it's the same as when you left, and I want to meet Tina and the boys. And besides, I want to see you so I can explain the letters, and I'm sorry I haven't made the trip out to see you."

Now JD was ashamed of himself. It was because of Charlie that his life was so good. JD said, "Well, in about a week and a half, we will be going to Oklahoma City to visit Tina's folks. I am truly sorry we have not come to see you. How about we will spend a week with them then spend a week with you?"

Charlie said, "Sounds great. I will call you next week, and I will stop the letters. Bring them, okay?"

"Sure thing," JD said and hung up. He felt bad. You see, his uncle Charlie raised him. Uncle Charlie used to drink a lot. Once, he was out running around and raising hell—his wife and son were at home—his son was sick and died. That same night, his wife took a handful of Charlie's pills and killed herself. Charlie came home two days later and found them.

Well, Charlie sobered up a week after this happened. JD's mom and dad were killed in a car wreck; Charlie was there in an hour. He packed up all of JD's things and said, "Boy, you're going to live with me." JD was only three then.

As JD was approaching the house, he could see the pickup and a white picket fence going around the house. *Good*, he thought, *Uncle Charlie's home.*

Tina said, "Nice, handsome house." JD looked at the log home. It was the same as when he left but somehow different. He blew the horn twice. He was sure Charlie would come out to greet them, but no Charlie.

Tina said, "You think he's home?"

JD said, "Should be. The pickup's here unless he bought another one. Let's just go in, and I will show you the house."

They stepped into the living room, and it was like time went back to the 1800s. The fireplace was so large you could walk into it. Long guns and pistols were hanging on the walls, and something new—pictures of all the families that had lived there; some, JD knew. There were even pictures of his family. How did he get them? He looked at Tina. She smiled at him. "He called me one day and asked me to send them. But some are not what we took."

JD showed her the bedrooms; all had four post featherbeds. Then he told her, "Here is the bathroom. I had to hand-carry water in to take a bath," and as the door was opening, he said, "and if you need to—wow! A toilet and a whirlpool tub. What the . . . He must have put everything in, thinking I was coming back to settle down." He felt really bad now. In the kitchen, the old woodburning stove was still there, but the hand pump in the sink was gone; it had working water faucets now. There was a microwave on the counter and a modern frig with water and ice cubes in the door.

Off to the side of the kitchen, what Charlie called the eaten room that they never used, the big oak table was gone. In its place was a sofa and a recliner with TV trays beside them. In the corner was a big flat-screen TV with a cable box. "Wow!" JD said. "He went all out fixen' the place up like this."

They went back to the living room. Over in the corner on a table, JD saw a cell phone with a Post-it note on it. He walked over and picked it up. On the note, it said, "JD, call me." It had Franklin's phone number on it.

Tina was reading the note over JD's shoulder and said, "Who is that?"

JD said, "It's Charlie's friend and lawyer." He dialed the number.

Franklin answered and said, "Franklin here."

JD said, "This is JD. Is my uncle Charlie okay? Is he in the hospital or something?"

Franklin said, "JD, just call me Frank. I am sorry to tell you this, but we buried Charlie over a week ago. We had tried to contact you, but we couldn't reach you. We waited as long as we could."

JD said, "I forgot my phone at home, we been using Tina's phone. I called last week like we planned, but no answer."

Frank said, "Why don't you come to my office. I have some papers for you to sign and other things your uncle Charlie wanted me to give you. It can wait if need be. Are you in town?"

JD said, "Yes, we are, and I will be down in an hour or so. See you then."

When they got to Franklin's office, Franklin got up from his desk, walked over to JD, and gave him a hug. Franklin said, "Boy, you have changed. No longer a skinny boy, you filled out into a man. I am sorry about Charlie. We grew up together; he was my best friend. He had stopped by my office to ask me to draw up papers for you to take the ownership of the land and house. He gave me the keys to the truck, house, and all the safe-deposit boxes at the bank. There's a dozen of them. I also took care of all the papers you need to get in the boxes. Just go over and see Kevin, the bank manager and friend of your uncle's. He's taking it hard. All three of us were drinking buddies back in the day. Here's a letter he left for you."

The next day, after they went to the graveyard, they went to the bank. Kevin was waiting for them. Kevin ran up to JD with tears in his eyes and gave JD a hug. "Man, it is sure good to see you again. Your uncle Charlie loved the hell out of you. I sure am going to miss him," Kevin said. "He did so much for Frank and I, well hell, the people in this town.

They didn't know it, but anytime they couldn't pay a bill or needed food, your uncle Charlie would have me put money in their bank accounts. If asked where the deposit came from, I would tell them the Legacy Foundation made the deposit. No one knew the money came from Charlie. Charlie, Frank, and I would laugh when they called your Uncle, "Crazy Charlie." If only they knew. He helped Frank and I with college. I am sure you want to see the boxes."

JD said, "What's in them?"

Kevin looked at him and said, "You mean you don't know?"

"No," said JD.

Kevin said, "Let me take you back and show you. When your uncle showed us, Frank and I already knew. We helped him. Let me help you open the first one. While you are looking, I'll get Frank to come over. We need to talk." They got to the first box, and Kevin left.

JD and Tina opened the box and stared at the contents. It had all of his great-great-great-grandpa's pearl-handled six-shooters and a tin star in it. Also in the box were twenty- and fifty-dollar gold coins. Thousands of them, dating back to the 1800s.

From across the room, Frank said, "That gold was paid to one of your relatives from the gold that he sold to the Mint when we were in our teens. Kevin and I went with your uncle to the boulder. At that time, it still was as large as a car. But we chipped it little by little until it was in nuggets. Then when the boulder was gone, we thought, well, that's it; but behind the box canyon your house lay on, there was more gold just lying on top of the ground. There still is gold there. They opened the rest of the boxes, all filled with large bags of gold nuggets."

"And that's not all," Kevin said.

"There's more?" said JD.

"Yep," said Kevin.

Frank spoke up then and said, "Kevin has another letter for you that will explain the letters. Charlie was about to tell you over the phone. You see, he was in my office that day he called you and asked if you would come sign the papers. He told me to get the papers ready and call him when they were ready. Well, I called the next day. No answer. So I called later that night, again, no answer. I figured he was out in the canyon, so the next day, I stopped by. The truck was in the yard, so I thought he was here. He was sitting in his chair with the phone in his hand, your number on the screen, but he never pushed the button.

"Doc said his heart gave out. That's wild because just before you left, he found out he had the big C. He said he didn't want to tell you because the doc only gave him six months. He lasted five years. He said it was his job to take care of you, not you take care of him. That's why he came up with the plan for you to get your life started without him. He didn't want you to watch him die. He looked bad though."

Frank said, "Have you read all the letters?"

JD said, "No. We tried, but they didn't make any sense; some were written by Charlie; the others were in several different hands."

Frank said, "Yes, they were from your past relatives. They were letters from home, some from far-away lands, some were stories of their adventures. Do you remember when you were in the ninth grade, you had to write a story for class? It was about a dog who saved a town from a flood. Your uncle took it to the newspaper, and they printed it. Charlie was so proud of you. He just knew you would be a writer. There's enough to write a lot of books."

JD said, "Well, if I can get them in order."

Kevin said, "That's easy. If you take a page, look in the right-hand corner, you will see like C-2-7. C stands for Charlie; dash 2 means second letter; dash 7 means seven pages. Have you checked out the root cellar?"

Frank looked at Kevin and shook his head, no, then cleared his throat. Kevin looked at Frank and said, "Well, we helped Charlie dig it, but you go home, open the letter, and explore it yourself, it will blow your mind. So sign here. I have transferred all of Charlie's bank accounts into yours. Here's the amount transferred." He handed JD a piece of paper.

JD and Tina both stared at it then looked at each other. JD said, "Is this a joke?"

Kevin said, "No, there's a little over five million in your account, plus you have millions in gold in those boxes. If you write the books on your family history, no telling how much they could bring in, and if you go down . . ." Frank snapped and yelled,

"Kevin!" Kevin looked at Frank and said, "Just go home and read the letter."

So they headed for his log home. When they got there, they opened the letter. It read,

> JD, if you are reading this, that means I have passed on. I am sorry I didn't tell you I was sick, but I didn't want you to have the burden of having to bury a loved one; the loss is a lot to bear. I, in one year, had to bury my mom and dad, then my wife, and son, then your mom and dad. What I want you to feel is how good it is to pass on a legacy to your sons. It's not just the money and the gold, it's passing on family history. It will make you rich in your heart. So live life to the fullest. Live for today because tomorrow may never come. I will wait for you on the other side. Please take your time getting here. I love you, son. Now go to my closet. In the corner, on the floor, there looks like a knot in the wood. Press it and step back.

Tina and JD went to the closet. JD saw the knot in the corner. He pressed it and took a couple of steps back. He heard a *click, click*, then part of the floor started to rise. When the door was open, they looked down the stairs. A light came on at the bottom of the stairs. They went down, and when they were at the bottom, they were standing in a hand-dug room eight feet tall, forty feet wide, and a hundred feet deep. It was full of rows of twenty-gallon tin milk jugs.

JD had a flashback of when he was about ten years old. He went to an auction with his uncle Charlie, and he bought hundreds of milk jugs. People said he was crazy for buying milk jugs. But here they all were, in double-stacked rows. He went over to a jug and pulled the top off, it was full of gold. He reached out and put his hand on it and just smiled.

Years Later

JD was sitting on the porch thinking of an opening to start his next book. It would be about Uncle Charlie. He looked up to see his eldest son standing next to him. His son said, "Dad, would you buy me a dirt bike?"

JD said, "Well, you have to earn it by doing your chores and helping your mom with her garden."

"Earn it? I thought we were rich," said his son.

JD said, "Well, if we spend it now, what kind of a legacy will you pass on to your son?"

"Legacy," his son said. "What's that?"

JD smiled and said, "One day I will write you a letter to explain and send it to you."

His son said, "Are you going to write how your uncle died?"

JD said, "No, I am going to write about how he lived. I think I will call it *Charlie's Legacy*."

Time to Write

I look out my window; looks cold and gray.
They say no sunshine for a few days.
So here I sit with pen in hand,
Trying to think of anything I can.
There are days when any subject will do,
Then days like this one, when
you have the blues.
There are times when you
have plenty to write,
Then times when you got nothing;
you sit there all night.
You get that one ray of light that
breaks through the clouds,
Then you get that rush of
thoughts that seem so loud.
You don't want to write
something dark and cold.
You want to write something
uplifting and bold.
It takes a ray of sunshine to
put a smile on your face.

It seems to brighten up the
mood in this ole place.
At times I bitch and moan
about nothing to write,
But it's been there all along in plain sight.
Try to write about nothing to do.
It just might make you feel blue too.

Thing for Granted

Well, I like the smile on your face
Because it brightens up this old place.
And I love it when we're alone
In this place that we call home.
Well, it seems like it was yesterday
When we would go out to play.
You have always been my best friend;
Looks like we will be together till the end.
You've been a friend, a lover, now a wife.
I feel we will be together for life.
Then one day, you blew my world apart
When you said you needed a new start.
It didn't take long
Before you were packed and gone.
I was dazed and confused,
Just sitting here missing you.
Weeks went by,
But I didn't cry.
You can love someone till it hurts,
Then you wonder, did I do
wrong? Was I a jerk?

I do not question why;
I feel the blues, I can't lie.
Then the phone rang late one night,
You told me the number of your flight.
Well, that was music to my ears;
It melted away all my fears.
I never asked where you went.
I imagined it was time well spent.
Now you've been home for a while
With that great big smile.
Just remember when you take
things for granted,
It doesn't always turn out like you planned it.

Child Support Blues

I drink rye whiskey and take
a handful of pills
Just so I can pay the damned ole bills.
I don't want to be a child-support bum,
But in order to work, I got to feel numb.
I pay a mortgage on a house
and three used cars;
That's about right for me, I'm up to par.
Ex number one is still pretty mad
'Cause they repossessed everything we had.
Ex number two said, "Don't get
my sister drunk again,
Because she wakes up naked and confused
and don't know where she's been."
Ex number three, well, she's just as crazy.
I pay for her house, and she still calls me lazy.
I have no money, these gals
just don't understand.
My choice for dinner is bologna or ham.
Now Christmas is coming; I
have to buy for eight kids.

Time to sell my gun collection.
Do I have any bids?
Hell, three kids aren't even mine;
These gals think I'm blind.
Looks like I have to pay for 12 more years.
Time to go cheap and change
from whiskey to beer.
I wonder what I can pawn today.
Well, I don't need that deep fryer anyway.

Ex

Traveling this road we call life,
Just thinking about my ex-wife.
It's funny how I miss her this time of year.
I remember the fighting, then
we would shed tears.
But it's been three lonely years.
I do miss her; I wish she was here.
Why can't we just forgive and forget
The mistakes that we both have regrets?
People tell me I'll get over it.
I've been trying, but I haven't yet.
I still wish that she was here.
She says, "Why can't we just be friends?"
But she knows I'll love her until the end.
Even if there's a little doubt,
Why can't we just work things out?
To another, soon, she will belong.
I must travel this road alone,
Hoping my future will change
and be so bright,
Traveling down this road of life.

Silver Cup

Drinking life from a silver cup,
Sometimes sour, but I drink it up.
Sometimes life can be fun;
Other times, it can weigh a ton.
It's rough at times to make ends meet,
But you do what you have to
do to make life complete.
There are loves that fade in and out,
But end up one-night stands, no doubt.
Life can be a whirlwind of drama,
Streaking through space like a comet.
Drinking life from a silver cup,
Sometimes sour, but I drink it up.
My dreams take money; at times, it's tight.
That's when my dreams fog
and fade out of sight.
But my dreams come back
like the morning sun,
So fresh and bright, I know
my day has just begun.
Once I ran a race and won a silver cup,

Bright and shiny. I yelled,
"Hey, life, what's up?"
Drinking life from a silver cup,
Sometimes sour, but I drink it up.
So when you're down and out,
and life is a little rough,
Look over at that silver cup.
Just put it to your lips and tilt it up.

Broken Halos

Broken halos and shattered dreams,
You know exactly what I mean.
You were an angel in my eyes
Until you told all those lies.
We started our relationship on a good note,
But soon it's like crossing a
river in a leaking boat.
You said you wanted to be with
me forever and ever,
But I have to tell you, you're not very clever.
At first, I didn't look at you as a gold digger,
But your problems followed you, and
they became bigger and bigger.
You invited yourself along for the ride;
I couldn't say no, but I felt
disgust I couldn't hide.
It was like a show; I had to
let you play it out.
At this point, I had to let you go, no doubt.
I feel guilty for feeling this way,
But I sure can't wait another day.

You were an angel with such sweet dreams,
But now they seem broken and shattered,
You know what I mean.
Looks like I have to pay for
twelve more years.
Time to go cheap and change
from whiskey to beer.
I wonder what I can pawn today.
Well, I don't need that deep fryer anyway.

Boy Warrior

To my grandson and the boys and girls who join to become men and women who protect this country, I thank you for your service.

I watched him as he went out
to play with the boys.
They would have so much fun
playing with their toys.
Now he stands so proud and tall,
Says he wants to answer the call.
He says there are many who
fight for you and me.
I want to thank them by joining
the fight to be free.
He left a boy warrior to join an army of one.
He knows his boot camp and
training will not be fun.
So he is with his brothers-in-arms
And learning to fight to keep us from harm.
I watched him grow from a
boy into a young man.

He told me, "Grandpa, this has
always been my plan."
He will put his life on the line
with an army of one.
He will fight with pride and
honor and, yes, even a gun.
That's why I'm proud to say
He is my grandson!

Lyrics to songs

I'll Be Just Fine

Whiskey and wine have clouded my mind,
But I tell myself I'll be just fine.
Trying to think where things went wrong,
But there were things that didn't belong.
Like those phone calls late at night;
It's just a friend, isn't that all right?
You said you were out with the girls
In your best dress with your
high-dollar pearls.
Whiskey and wine have clouded my mind,
But I tell myself I'll be just fine.
You're a city girl that's given me the blues.
I'm a country boy whose just been used.
You took my love right from the start
Then took my heart and tore it apart.
Whiskey and wine have clouded my mind,
But I tell myself I'll be just fine.
I won't spend the rest of my days
Looking at the world through
a whiskey haze.
Time to sober up and find a country girl

Who'll be true and wants to share my world.
I'll lock your memory with
the whiskey and wine
In the back of my mind,
hoping never to find.
Whiskey and wine have clouded my mind,
But I tell myself I'll be just fine.

Funny

That day in the park, on bended knee,
I asked would you spend your life with me.
Our time together, I will never forget.
Life with you, yes, I had regrets
I guess I am funny, it's easy to see,
'Cause I care for a woman
who doesn't care for me.
Well, I woke up this morning;
You were nowhere in sight,
Then I remembered the fight
We had last night.
I said I was sorry; you said you were bored.
I watched you pack, then you
went out of the door.
I guess I am funny, it's easy to see,
'Cause I care for a woman
who doesn't care for me.
Looking out my window at the pouring rain,
Watching raindrops upon my windowpane.
This pain of losing you won't go away.
I think of you every single day.

I guess I am funny, it's easy to see,
'Cause I care for a woman
who doesn't care for me.
My mind is flooded with your memories;
Can't force you to love me, that's plain to see.
A reminder of a love that did not last;
Time to move on, can't live in the past.

Black Bird

A solitaire black bird sitting
on the upper rail,
A solitaire black bird sitting
on the upper rail,
He's just sitting there all alone
'Cause he has no place to call home.
A solitaire black bird sitting
on the upper rail,
Just waiting on an old man to
come walking down the trail,
Just waiting on an old man to
come walking down the trail.
He comes here just to feed me.
He doesn't want anyone to see.
A solitaire black bird sitting
on the upper rail.
I like the time that we spend alone.
I like the time that we spend alone.
He tells me how he lost his wife
And how much she was a part of his life.

A solitaire black bird sitting
on the upper rail.
The government sent his son off to war.
The government sent his son off to war.
His son lost his life in this war.
He hated the government; this he swore.
A solitaire black bird sitting
on the upper rail,
It's a burden of guilt is why I stay,
It's a burden of guilt is why I stay.
To watch this man pray every single day,
There's not much more that I can say;
A solitaire black bird sitting
on the upper rail.

About the Author

Joe Al Green is a man in his sixties. He has a wife, Carole, that he has been with for almost forty years. They have two kids, Joe and Melissa, who have given them grandkids and, now, great-grandkids. He owns a house he and his wife built on their own land in the country outside a small town in Oklahoma. He has two living brothers and three sisters. He has lost a sister, a brother, his dad, and his mom. At a young age, Joe had problems with alcohol and drugs and the law. At sixteen, he dropped out of high school, got a GED, had his mom and dad sign for him to go into the navy so he could fill a man's shoes. He did his tour in the navy, but his problems did not go away. He was a jack of all trades. He always got paid good and excelled in everything he did. But truck-driving was his passion. Somewhere around the age of thirty, after a weekend binge, he awoke with a drug hangover. He went to the mirror and looked at himself. He knew he needed to make a change, so he did. From that day on, he left his problems behind and got his life on the right track. Things went well until his mom's death. After thirty-five years and five million miles over the road, he had a heart attack that forced him into retirement. When his mom died, in a moment of grief, he wrote his first poem. All his work comes from the heart, thus the title of his book, Words from the Heart. He feels writing from the heart can touch you and leave you with a tear in your eye or a smile on your face

CPSIA information can be obtained
at www.ICGtesting.com
Printed in the USA
LVHW020905240620
658558LV00003B/18